JOURNEY TO BECOMING YOUR BEST SELF

TIANA SHARP

Before you start:

First I want to say Congratulations...
**for taking the first step towards
a better you.**

You should be proud of yourself.
And I am honored to help guide
you along your journey.

This Journal is:

- A safe space for your thoughts
- A space for self-discovery
- A place for reflection
- A place for you to be vulnerable
- A reminder for you to practice self-care
- A tool to help you make sense of your thoughts & the world
- Daily wellness check-in

This section of the book serves as self reflection of where you are at physically, emotionally, and mentally in your life. The first step towards personal growth is being honest with yourself.

You cannot heal what you won't reveal.

- Jay Z

I am the author of my own *life story*. I can start a new chapter anytime I choose.

At this exact moment in time who am I? What am I feeling?

Who do I want to become?

My Truths

Love is...?

Love is not...?

I deserve...?

Despite...?

My joys in life...?

Outweighs...?

What in my life gives me a sense of purpose and fills me with passion?

What areas in my life do I need to work on in order to become my best self?

Make a list of everything I've been expecting
of myself recently. All the things I worry about
that I feel like " I Should" be doing...

E
X
P
E
C
T
A
T
I
O
N
S

Read through your list and ask yourself are these
reasonable for ME? What can you cross off this
list now and forever?

What are five fears that are preventing me from
progressing in life?

"

Unrealistic expectations derive from the idea that we aren't good enough just the way we are. "When we live this way, we never fully live in the moments of our lives; we live in the sorrow of what wasn't and the fear of never being."

Jenn Fieldman

Get clear on my **Values.**
Quiet my fear.
I AM ENOUGH.

Give yourself your flowers. List 3 of your greatest strengths.

SQUAD CHECK

Who shows up for you?
Decorate your squad's jerseys

Who do I choose to surrond myself with?

In what ways do they show up for me?

Do they inspire with me or drain me? And how?

SQUAD CHECK

Who shows up for you?
Decorate your squad's jerseys

Who do I choose to surrond myself with?

In what ways do they show up for me?

Do they inspire with me or drain me? And how?

My **mental health** is more important than a career, money, and other people's opinions and expectations.

If taking care of myself means letting someone down, then I will let someone down.

What parts of myself and my life do I want to protect
in order to maintain my inner peace?

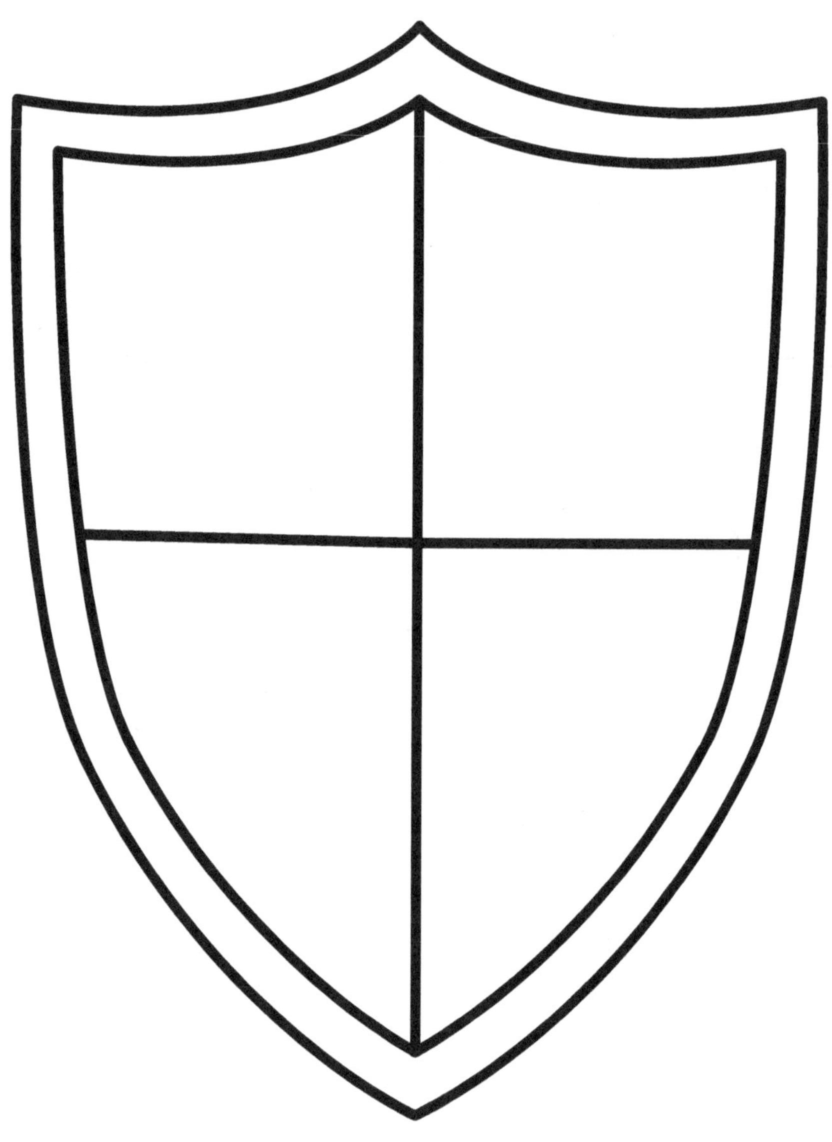

When you have some time head over to
https://www.16personalities.com/personality-types
and take their personality assessment.

It is completely **free** to take the test and get
your results. It will give you an amazingly
detailed insight of who you are and how you
navigate through life. Remember to be open and
honest while giving your answers and when
analyzing your results think about what
resonates true for you.
Using this tool will help you...

1. Understand your strengths and weaknesses
2. Deepen your relationships
3. Kick-start or navigate your career

What did you learn about yourself that surprised you or that you did not realize about yourself?

What was your take away from the test and how can you use what you learned to help you going forward?

This next section of the book will focus on helping you observe your feelings without judgment and help you start to build up your self-care routine.

Reset. Readjust. Refocus. As many times as I need to.

UNKNOWN

My Inner Battery

What activities and interactions drain me mentally and emotionally?

What boundaries can I set to save me from being drained?

What activities and interactions recharge my inner battery and give me energy?

How can I try to integrate more of these into my daily life?

How full is my battery right now?

(Shade in the battery according to
how you feel at the moment.)

Emotionally?   Physically?

What might I be in need of to help you recharge?

For my body?

For my mind?

IT"S MY PARTY AND I'LL CRY IF I WANT TO!

It is okay to not be okay all the time. I will let myself feel whatever you are feeling and show myself compassion and understanding. For the hard days what's on the agenda?...

Party Agenda

Location:

Soundtrack:

Dress Attire:

On the Menu: (Favorite Meal/Snack)

Self Care Activity :

Movie Choice:

My Thought Replacement Playlist

<table>
<tr><td align="center">Negative Thought
Playlist</td><td align="center">Positive Thought
Playlist</td></tr>
<tr><td>EX: I am lazy and that is why I am not successful like my peers.</td><td>EX: I have accomplished a lot and I will not measure my success against someone else's.</td></tr>
</table>

Your Inner Critic Affirmations

My inner critic is NOT a reflection of reality.

I am doing the best I can given my circumstances.

Change takes time, you cannot rush it, which involves patience.

I am worthy of love and validation.

Just because it's hard doesn't mean I am failing. I am not less for making mistakes and I give myself the space to learn from them and grow.

I am capable of amazing things.

I respect my limitations and recognize the abundance of capabilities I do possess

My strength is greater than any struggle.

I will make *myself* a priority, at the end of the day I am my longest commitment.

UNKNOWN

With This Promise Ring
I Promise...

What do I want to promise myself? How am I planning to promise to treat myself with kindness, compassion, & patience?

I Promise...

I Promise...

I Promise...

I Promise...

Self Care Morning Routine

Get up an hour before I
need to start my day

10 minute stretch
& meditation

Instead of checking my phone first thing in the morning
try listening to my favorite podcast or audiobook

 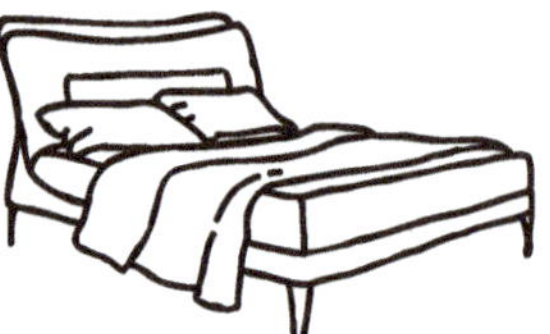

Gratitude Journaling

Make my Bed

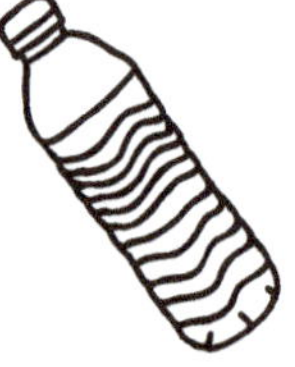 

Hydrate

Skincare routine

SELF LOVE

Soundtrack

What songs do I play when I need some TLC and calm
me down after a long day?

-
-
-
-
-
-
-
-
-
-
-
-
-

Scan the picture on the Spotify app to take a look at what's on my playlist!

DANCE
Soundtrack

What songs do I play when I want to dance like no one is watching? When I can be silly and and carefree?

-
-
-
-
-
-
-
-
-
-
-
-
-
-
-
-

Scan the picture on the Spotify app to take a look at what's on my playlist!

IM WINNING

Soundtrack

What songs make me feel like I can handle anything
life throws at me put me in a good mood

-
-
-
-
-
-
-
-
-
-
-
-
-
-

Scan the picture
on the Spotify app
to take a look at
what's on my
playlist!

NOSTALGIA
Soundtrack

What songs do I play when I want to remember...

-
-
-
-
-
-
-
-
-
-
-
-
-
-
-

Scan the picture
on the Spotify app
to take a look at
what's on my
playlist!

Self-care is giving the
world the *best* of you,
instead of what's *left* of
you.

KATIE REED

Realistic Social Media Detox

1. Know your boundaries

Social media can be awesome and fun to use but it is important to use it wisely and remember to unplug every now and then.

2. Structure your time on social media...

This will help you avoid zombie scrolling (scrolling for hours on end.) You don't have to quit social media cold turkey. Instead be aware of how much time you are spending on social media and set some time aside (30 mins to 2 hrs only) in your day AFTER your daily priorities are handled to enjoy social media. You will be surprised how much not using social media all throughout your day can help you be more productive and engaged with life

3. Block negative people & accounts

It is super important to be mindful of what your social media feed is FEEDING you. Are the accounts you follow feeding your depression or insecurities? If after scrolling on social media you feel drained, triggered, unhappy, and mentally exhausted you need to consider which accounts/people you are giving your time to unnecessarily.

4. Follow inspiring accounts

If social media is no longer fun for you or a place that invokes happiness and leisure, you are doing it wrong. Find accounts and people that align with your goals and who you want to be in life. This will motivate you, educate you on things you are interested in and energize you to take action.

MY SELF CARE LIBRARY

That book I never get
tired of reading: _______________________

The new Fictional book
I read for pleasure: _______________________

The book I read to advance
my Personal Growth: _______________________

The Self Help book I buy to help me
solve a problem I have been having: _______________________

A book you find that can give
you a new perspective on life: _______________________

Basic Plan

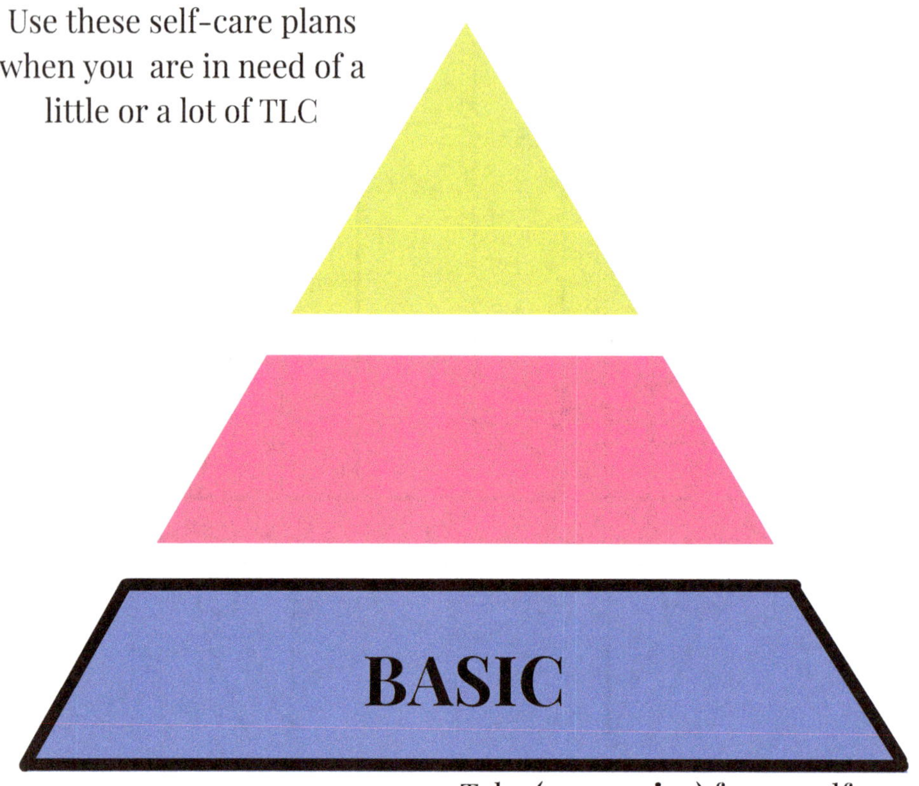

Take **(10-45 mins)** for myself

Small acts I can do that will bring me joy right now:

Some kind words for myself that I could use right now:

Deluxe Plan

Use these self-care plans
when you are in need of a
little or a lot of TLC

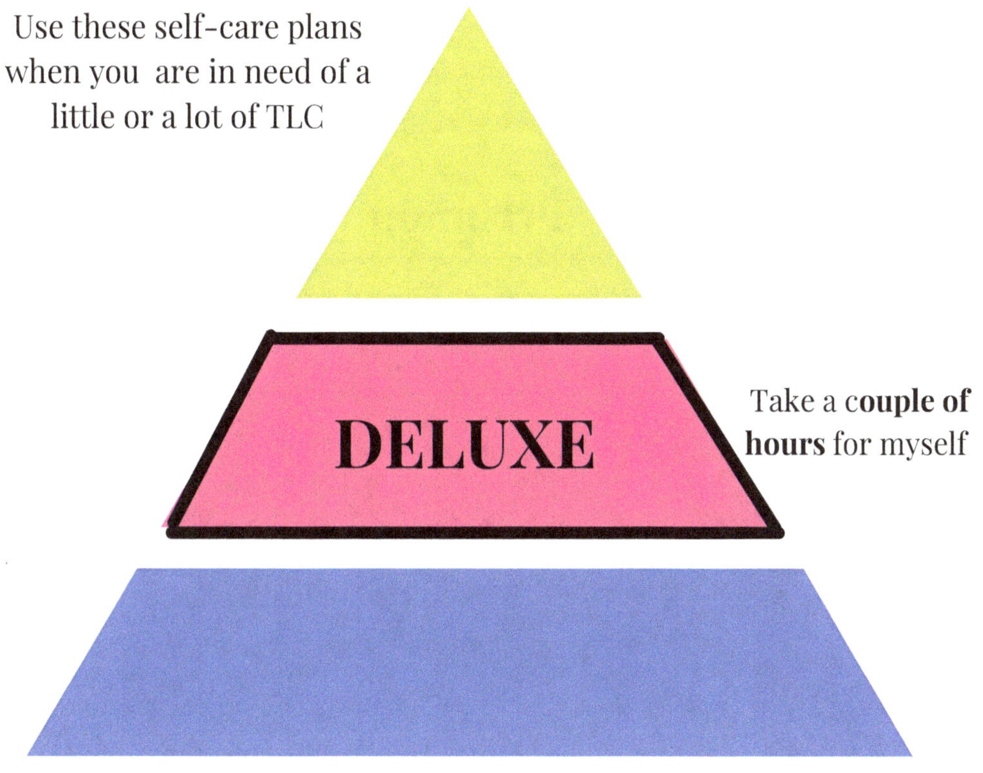

Activties I can do that will help me get out of my head for a while:

Comfort foods that would help my mood:

Premium Plan

Use these self-care plans
when you are in need of
a little or a lot of TLC

Take a **Whole Day**
for myself

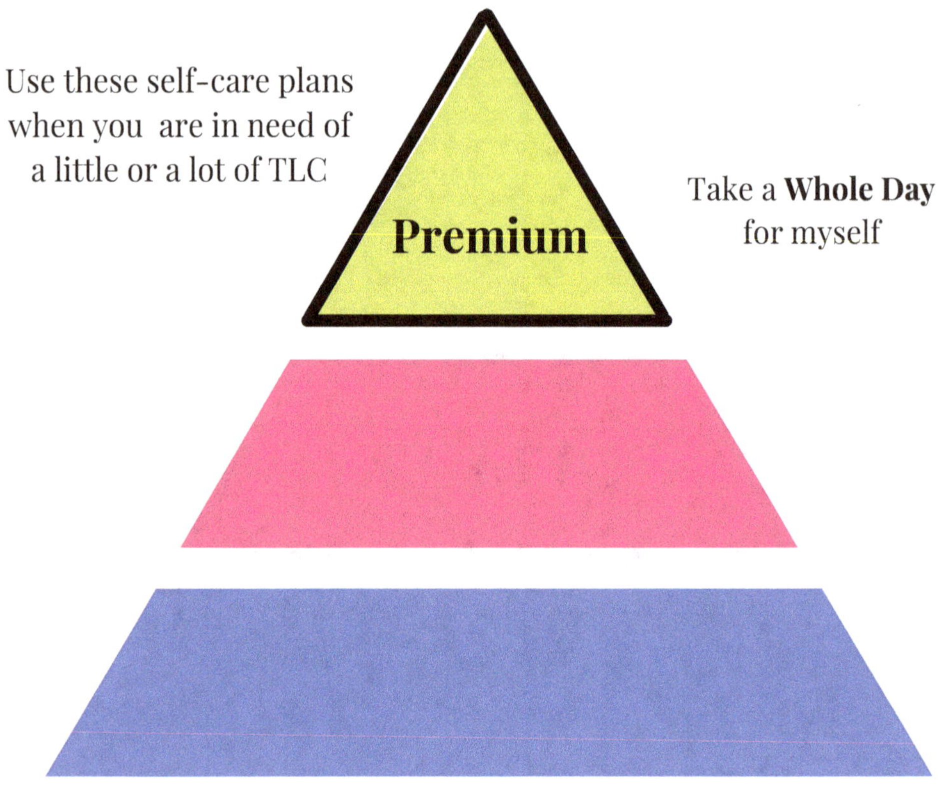

Spend some time with the people who I can count on:

6 Activities that I love to do the most:

* ________________________   * ________________________

* ________________________   * ________________________

* ________________________   * ________________________

THINGS I WANTED TO SAY BUT NEVER DID

Has there ever been a time where something/someone bothered or upset me, and I kept my mouth shut and ignored how I was feeling for the sake of other people's feelings. What do I wish I had said?

THINGS I WANTED TO SAY BUT NEVER DID

Has there ever been a time where something/someone bothered or upset me, and I kept my mouth shut and ignored how I was feeling for the sake of other people's feelings. What do I wish I had said?

A LETTER TO MY CHILDHOOD SELF

Dear Younger Me,

A LETTER TO MY FUTURE SELF

Dear Future Me,

This next section of the book is a 30 day Self Care Planner that serves to help you prioritize your problems and concerns and manage the stress & anxieties of daily life so you can **CALM THE CHAOS** by practicing daily reflection and forming better self-care habits.

30 DAY MOOD TRACKER

1	2	3	4	5
6	7	8	9	10
11	12	13	14	15
16	17	18	19	20
21	22	23	24	25
26	27	28	29	30

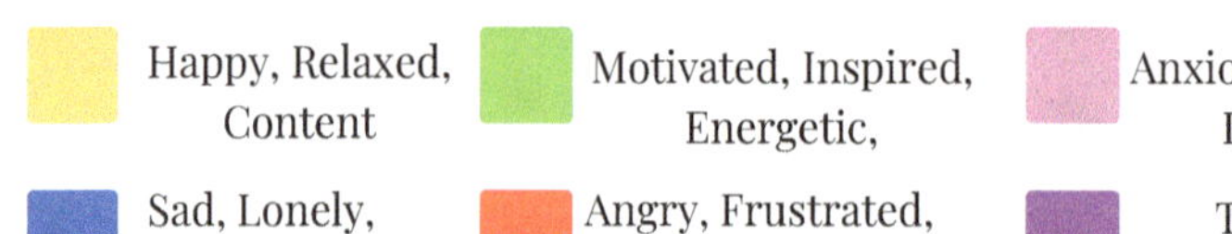

DATE:

Sun   M   T   W   Th   F   Sat

MANIFEST:

WATER INTAKE: (SHADE IN)

3 THINGS I AM GRATEFUL FOR TODAY:

1.
2.
3.

THINGS I NEED TO DO FOR ME TODAY

1.
2.
3.

THINGS TO GET DONE:

Achieved? ✔

CLEAN:

DAILY HABITS I WANT
    TO FORM:

Achieved? ✔

1.

2.

3.

4.

5.

PURCHASE:

3 PERSONAL WINS TODAY:

BRAIN DUMP & DAILY REFLECTION:

<table><tr><td>DATE:</td></tr><tr><td>Sun M T W Th F Sat</td></tr></table>

MANIFEST:

WATER INTAKE: (SHADE IN)

3 THINGS I AM GRATEFUL FOR TODAY:
1.
2.
3.

TODAY"S PRIORITIES:
1.
2.
3.

THINGS I NEED TO DO FOR ME TODAY
1.
2.
3.

THINGS TO GET DONE:
Achieved? ✔

CLEAN:

DAILY HABITS I WANT
TO FORM:
Achieved? ✔
1.
2.
3.
4.
5.

PURCHASE:

3 PERSONAL WINS TODAY:

BRAIN DUMP & DAILY REFLECTION:

DATE:

Sun M T W Th F Sat

MANIFEST:

WATER INTAKE: (SHADE IN)

3 THINGS I AM GRATEFUL FOR TODAY:

1.
2.
3.

THINGS I NEED TO DO FOR ME TODAY

1.
2.
3.

THINGS TO GET DONE:

Achieved? ✔

CLEAN:

DAILY HABITS I WANT
   TO FORM:

Achieved? ✔

1.

2.

3.

4.

5.

PURCHASE:

3 PERSONAL WINS TODAY:

BRAIN DUMP & DAILY REFLECTION:

DATE:

Sun M T W Th F Sat

MANIFEST:

WATER INTAKE: (SHADE IN)

3 THINGS I AM GRATEFUL FOR TODAY:

1.
2.
3.

TODAY"S PRIORITIES:

1.
2.
3.

THINGS I NEED TO DO FOR ME TODAY

1.
2.
3.

THINGS TO GET DONE:

Achieved? ✔

CLEAN:

DAILY HABITS I WANT
TO FORM:

Achieved? ✔

1.

2.

3.

4.

5.

PURCHASE:

3 PERSONAL WINS TODAY:

BRAIN DUMP & DAILY REFLECTION:

How full is my battery right now?

(Shade in the battery according to
how you feel at the moment.)

Emotionally? Physically?

What might I be in need of to help me recharge?

For my body?

For my mind?

DATE:

Sun M T W Th F Sat

MANIFEST:

WATER INTAKE: (SHADE IN)

3 THINGS I AM GRATEFUL FOR TODAY:

1.
2.
3.

TODAY"S PRIORITIES:

1.
2.
3.

THINGS I NEED TO DO FOR ME TODAY

1.
2.
3.

THINGS TO GET DONE:

Achieved? ✔

CLEAN:

DAILY HABITS I WANT
   TO FORM:

Achieved? ✔

1.

2.

3.

4.

5.

PURCHASE:

3 PERSONAL WINS TODAY:

BRAIN DUMP & DAILY REFLECTION:

DATE:

Sun M T W Th F Sat

MANIFEST:

WATER INTAKE: (SHADE IN)

3 THINGS I AM GRATEFUL FOR TODAY:
1.
2.
3.

TODAY"S PRIORITIES:
1.
2.
3.

THINGS I NEED TO DO FOR ME TODAY
1.
2.
3.

THINGS TO GET DONE:
Achieved? ✔

CLEAN:

DAILY HABITS I WANT
    TO FORM:
Achieved? ✔
1.
2.
3.
4.
5.

PURCHASE:

3 PERSONAL WINS TODAY:

BRAIN DUMP & DAILY REFLECTION:

DATE:

Sun M T W Th F Sat

MANIFEST:

WATER INTAKE: (SHADE IN)

3 THINGS I AM GRATEFUL FOR TODAY:

1.
2.
3.

TODAY"S PRIORITIES:

1.
2.
3.

THINGS I NEED TO DO FOR ME TODAY

1.
2.
3.

THINGS TO GET DONE:

Achieved? ✔

CLEAN:

DAILY HABITS I WANT TO FORM:

Achieved? ✔

1.

2.

3.

4.

5.

PURCHASE:

3 PERSONAL WINS TODAY:

BRAIN DUMP & DAILY REFLECTION:

<table><tr><td>DATE:</td></tr><tr><td>Sun M T W Th F Sat</td></tr></table>

MANIFEST:

WATER INTAKE: (SHADE IN)

3 THINGS I AM GRATEFUL FOR TODAY:

1.
2.
3.

TODAY"S PRIORITIES:

1.
2.
3.

THINGS I NEED TO DO FOR ME TODAY

1.
2.
3.

THINGS TO GET DONE:

Achieved? ✔

CLEAN:

DAILY HABITS I WANT TO FORM:

Achieved? ✔

1.
2.
3.
4.
5.

PURCHASE:

3 PERSONAL WINS TODAY:

BRAIN DUMP & DAILY REFLECTION:

DATE:

| Sun | M | T | W | Th | F | Sat |

MANIFEST:

WATER INTAKE: (SHADE IN)

3 THINGS I AM GRATEFUL FOR TODAY:
1.
2.
3.

TODAY"S PRIORITIES:
1.
2.
3.

THINGS I NEED TO DO FOR ME TODAY

1.
2.
3.

THINGS TO GET DONE:

Achieved? ✔

CLEAN:

DAILY HABITS I WANT
TO FORM:

Achieved? ✔
1.
2.
3.
4.
5.

PURCHASE:

3 PERSONAL WINS TODAY:

BRAIN DUMP & DAILY REFLECTION:

<table><tr><td>DATE:</td></tr><tr><td>Sun M T W Th F Sat</td></tr></table>

MANIFEST:

WATER INTAKE: (SHADE IN)

3 THINGS I AM GRATEFUL FOR TODAY:

1.
2.
3.

THINGS I NEED TO DO FOR ME TODAY

1.
2.
3.

THINGS TO GET DONE:

Achieved? ✔

CLEAN:

DAILY HABITS I WANT TO FORM:

Achieved? ✔

1.

2.

3.

4.

5.

PURCHASE:

3 PERSONAL WINS TODAY:

BRAIN DUMP & DAILY REFLECTION:

How full is my battery right now?

(Shade in the battery according to
how you feel at the moment.)

Emotionally?   Physically?

What might I be in need of to help me recharge?

For my body?

For my mind?

DATE:

Sun   M   T   W   Th   F   Sat

MANIFEST:

WATER INTAKE: (SHADE IN)

3 THINGS I AM GRATEFUL FOR TODAY:

1.
2.
3.

TODAY"S PRIORITIES:

1.
2.
3.

THINGS I NEED TO DO FOR ME TODAY

1.
2.
3.

THINGS TO GET DONE:

Achieved? ✔

CLEAN:

DAILY HABITS I WANT
TO FORM:

Achieved? ✔

1.

2.

3.

4.

5.

PURCHASE:

3 PERSONAL WINS TODAY:

BRAIN DUMP & DAILY REFLECTION:

DATE:

Sun M T W Th F Sat

MANIFEST:

WATER INTAKE: (SHADE IN)

3 THINGS I AM GRATEFUL FOR TODAY:

1.
2.
3.

TODAY"S PRIORITIES:

1.
2.
3.

THINGS I NEED TO DO FOR ME TODAY

1.
2.
3.

THINGS TO GET DONE:

Achieved? ✔

CLEAN:

DAILY HABITS I WANT TO FORM:

Achieved? ✔

1.
2.
3.
4.
5.

PURCHASE:

3 PERSONAL WINS TODAY:

BRAIN DUMP & DAILY REFLECTION:

<table>
<tr><td>DATE:

Sun M T W Th F Sat</td><td>MANIFEST:</td></tr>
</table>

MANIFEST:

WATER INTAKE: (SHADE IN)

3 THINGS I AM GRATEFUL FOR TODAY:

1.
2.
3.

TODAY"S PRIORITIES:

1.
2.
3.

THINGS I NEED TO DO FOR ME TODAY

1.
2.
3.

THINGS TO GET DONE:

Achieved? ✔

CLEAN:

PURCHASE:

DAILY HABITS I WANT TO FORM:

Achieved? ✔

1.
2.
3.
4.
5.

3 PERSONAL WINS TODAY:

BRAIN DUMP & DAILY REFLECTION:

DATE:

Sun M T W Th F Sat

MANIFEST:

WATER INTAKE: (SHADE IN)

3 THINGS I AM GRATEFUL FOR TODAY:
1.
2.
3.

TODAY"S PRIORITIES:
1.
2.
3.

THINGS I NEED TO DO FOR ME TODAY
1.
2.
3.

THINGS TO GET DONE:

Achieved? ✔

CLEAN:

PURCHASE:

DAILY HABITS I WANT TO FORM:

Achieved? ✔
1.
2.
3.
4.
5.

3 PERSONAL WINS TODAY:

BRAIN DUMP & DAILY REFLECTION:

<table><tr><td>DATE:</td></tr><tr><td>Sun M T W Th F Sat</td></tr></table>

MANIFEST:

WATER INTAKE: (SHADE IN)

3 THINGS I AM GRATEFUL FOR TODAY:

1.
2.
3.

TODAY"S PRIORITIES:

1.
2.
3.

THINGS I NEED TO DO FOR ME TODAY

1.
2.
3.

THINGS TO GET DONE:

Achieved? ✔

CLEAN:

PURCHASE:

DAILY HABITS I WANT TO FORM:

Achieved? ✔

1.
2.
3.
4.
5.

3 PERSONAL WINS TODAY:

BRAIN DUMP & DAILY REFLECTION:

DATE:

Sun M T W Th F Sat

MANIFEST:

WATER INTAKE: (SHADE IN)

3 THINGS I AM GRATEFUL FOR TODAY:

1.
2.
3.

TODAY"S PRIORITIES:

1.
2.
3.

THINGS I NEED TO DO FOR ME TODAY

1.
2.
3.

THINGS TO GET DONE:

Achieved? ✔

CLEAN:

PURCHASE:

DAILY HABITS I WANT TO FORM:

Achieved? ✔

1.
2.
3.
4.
5.

3 PERSONAL WINS TODAY:

BRAIN DUMP & DAILY REFLECTION:

How full is my battery right now?

(Shade in the battery according to
how you feel at the moment.)

Emotionally?   Physically?

What might I be in need of to help me recharge?

For my body?

For my mind?

DATE:

Sun M T W Th F Sat

MANIFEST:

WATER INTAKE: (SHADE IN)

3 THINGS I AM GRATEFUL FOR TODAY:
1.
2.
3.

TODAY"S PRIORITIES:
1.
2.
3.

THINGS I NEED TO DO FOR ME TODAY
1.
2.
3.

THINGS TO GET DONE:
Achieved? ✔

CLEAN:

DAILY HABITS I WANT
TO FORM:
Achieved? ✔
1.
2.
3.
4.
5.

PURCHASE:

3 PERSONAL WINS TODAY:

BRAIN DUMP & DAILY REFLECTION:

DATE:

Sun   M   T   W   Th   F   Sat

MANIFEST:

WATER INTAKE: (SHADE IN)

3 THINGS I AM GRATEFUL FOR TODAY:

1.
2.
3.

TODAY"S PRIORITIES:

1.
2.
3.

THINGS I NEED TO DO FOR ME TODAY

1.
2.
3.

THINGS TO GET DONE:

Achieved? ✔

CLEAN:

DAILY HABITS I WANT
TO FORM:

Achieved? ✔

1.

2.

3.

4.

5.

PURCHASE:

3 PERSONAL WINS TODAY:

BRAIN DUMP & DAILY REFLECTION:

DATE:

Sun M T W Th F Sat

MANIFEST:

WATER INTAKE: (SHADE IN)

3 THINGS I AM GRATEFUL FOR TODAY:

1.
2.
3.

TODAY"S PRIORITIES:

1.
2.
3.

THINGS I NEED TO DO FOR ME TODAY

1.
2.
3.

THINGS TO GET DONE:

Achieved?✔

CLEAN:

DAILY HABITS I WANT
   TO FORM:

Achieved?✔

1.

2.

3.

4.

5.

PURCHASE:

3 PERSONAL WINS TODAY:

BRAIN DUMP & DAILY REFLECTION:

DATE:

Sun M T W Th F Sat

MANIFEST:

WATER INTAKE: (SHADE IN)

3 THINGS I AM GRATEFUL FOR TODAY:

1.
2.
3.

TODAY"S PRIORITIES:

1.
2.
3.

THINGS I NEED TO DO FOR ME TODAY

1.
2.
3.

THINGS TO GET DONE:

Achieved? ✔

CLEAN:

DAILY HABITS I WANT
TO FORM:

Achieved? ✔

1.

2.

3.

4.

PURCHASE:

5.

3 PERSONAL WINS TODAY:

BRAIN DUMP & DAILY REFLECTION:

DATE:

Sun M T W Th F Sat

MANIFEST:

WATER INTAKE: (SHADE IN)

3 THINGS I AM GRATEFUL FOR TODAY:
1.
2.
3.

TODAY"S PRIORITIES:
1.
2.
3.

THINGS I NEED TO DO FOR ME TODAY
1.
2.
3.

THINGS TO GET DONE:
Achieved? ✔

CLEAN:

DAILY HABITS I WANT
TO FORM:
Achieved? ✔
1.
2.
3.
4.
5.

PURCHASE:

3 PERSONAL WINS TODAY:

BRAIN DUMP & DAILY REFLECTION:

DATE:

Sun M T W Th F Sat

MANIFEST:

WATER INTAKE: (SHADE IN)

3 THINGS I AM GRATEFUL FOR TODAY:

1.
2.
3.

TODAY"S PRIORITIES:

1.
2.
3.

THINGS I NEED TO DO FOR ME TODAY

1.
2.
3.

THINGS TO GET DONE:

Achieved? ✔

CLEAN:

DAILY HABITS I WANT TO FORM:

Achieved? ✔

1.
2.
3.
4.
5.

PURCHASE:

3 PERSONAL WINS TODAY:

BRAIN DUMP & DAILY REFLECTION:

DATE:

Sun M T W Th F Sat

MANIFEST:

WATER INTAKE: (SHADE IN)

3 THINGS I AM GRATEFUL FOR TODAY:

1.
2.
3.

TODAY"S PRIORITIES:

1.
2.
3.

THINGS I NEED TO DO FOR ME TODAY

1.
2.
3.

THINGS TO GET DONE:

Achieved? ✔

CLEAN:

DAILY HABITS I WANT
    TO FORM:

Achieved? ✔

1.

2.

3.

4.

5.

PURCHASE:

3 PERSONAL WINS TODAY:

BRAIN DUMP & DAILY REFLECTION:

How full is my battery right now?

(Shade in the battery according to
how you feel at the moment.)

What might I be in need of to help me recharge?

For my body?

For my mind?

DATE:

Sun M T W Th F Sat

MANIFEST:

WATER INTAKE: (SHADE IN)

3 THINGS I AM GRATEFUL FOR TODAY:

1.
2.
3.

TODAY"S PRIORITIES:

1.
2.
3.

THINGS I NEED TO DO FOR ME TODAY

1.
2.
3.

THINGS TO GET DONE:

Achieved? ✔

CLEAN:

DAILY HABITS I WANT
   TO FORM:

Achieved? ✔

1.

2.

3.

4.

5.

PURCHASE:

3 PERSONAL WINS TODAY:

BRAIN DUMP & DAILY REFLECTION:

<table><tr><td>DATE:</td></tr><tr><td>Sun M T W Th F Sat</td></tr></table>

MANIFEST:

WATER INTAKE: (SHADE IN)

3 THINGS I AM GRATEFUL FOR TODAY:
1.
2.
3.

TODAY"S PRIORITIES:
1.
2.
3.

THINGS I NEED TO DO FOR ME TODAY
1.
2.
3.

THINGS TO GET DONE:
Achieved? ✔

CLEAN:

PURCHASE:

DAILY HABITS I WANT TO FORM:
Achieved? ✔
1.
2.
3.
4.
5.

3 PERSONAL WINS TODAY:

BRAIN DUMP & DAILY REFLECTION:

DATE:

Sun M T W Th F Sat

MANIFEST:

WATER INTAKE: (SHADE IN)

3 THINGS I AM GRATEFUL FOR TODAY:

1.
2.
3.

TODAY"S PRIORITIES:

1.
2.
3.

THINGS I NEED TO DO FOR ME TODAY

1.
2.
3.

THINGS TO GET DONE:

Achieved? ✔

CLEAN:

DAILY HABITS I WANT
TO FORM:

Achieved? ✔

1.

2.

3.

4.

PURCHASE:

5.

3 PERSONAL WINS TODAY:

BRAIN DUMP & DAILY REFLECTION:

<table>
<tr><td>

DATE:

Sun M T W Th F Sat

</td><td>

MANIFEST:

</td></tr>
</table>

WATER INTAKE: (SHADE IN)

3 THINGS I AM GRATEFUL FOR TODAY:

1.
2.
3.

TODAY"S PRIORITIES:

1.
2.
3.

THINGS I NEED TO DO FOR ME TODAY

1.
2.
3.

THINGS TO GET DONE:

Achieved? ✔

○
○
○

CLEAN:

○
○
○
○

PURCHASE:

○
○
○
○

DAILY HABITS I WANT TO FORM:

Achieved? ✔

1. ○
2. ○
3. ○
4. ○
5. ○

3 PERSONAL WINS TODAY:

BRAIN DUMP & DAILY REFLECTION:

DATE:

Sun M T W Th F Sat

MANIFEST:

WATER INTAKE: (SHADE IN)

3 THINGS I AM GRATEFUL FOR TODAY:
1.
2.
3.

TODAY"S PRIORITIES:
1.
2.
3.

THINGS I NEED TO DO FOR ME TODAY

1.
2.
3.

THINGS TO GET DONE:
Achieved? ✔

CLEAN:

DAILY HABITS I WANT
TO FORM:
Achieved? ✔
1.
2.
3.
4.
5.

PURCHASE:

3 PERSONAL WINS TODAY:

BRAIN DUMP & DAILY REFLECTION:

DATE:

Sun M   T   W   Th   F   Sat

MANIFEST:

WATER INTAKE: (SHADE IN)

3 THINGS I AM GRATEFUL FOR TODAY:

1.
2.
3.

TODAY"S PRIORITIES:

1.
2.
3.

THINGS I NEED TO DO FOR ME TODAY

1.
2.
3.

THINGS TO GET DONE:

Achieved? ✔

CLEAN:

PURCHASE:

DAILY HABITS I WANT
TO FORM:

Achieved? ✔

1.
2.
3.
4.
5.

3 PERSONAL WINS TODAY:

BRAIN DUMP & DAILY REFLECTION:

DATE:

| Sun | M | T | W | Th | F | Sat |

MANIFEST:

WATER INTAKE: (SHADE IN)

3 THINGS I AM GRATEFUL FOR TODAY:
1.
2.
3.

TODAY"S PRIORITIES:
1.
2.
3.

THINGS I NEED TO DO FOR ME TODAY

1.
2.
3.

THINGS TO GET DONE:
Achieved? ✔

CLEAN:

DAILY HABITS I WANT
TO FORM:
Achieved? ✔
1.
2.
3.
4.
5.

PURCHASE:

3 PERSONAL WINS TODAY:

BRAIN DUMP & DAILY REFLECTION:

DATE:

Sun M T W Th F Sat

MANIFEST:

WATER INTAKE: (SHADE IN)

3 THINGS I AM GRATEFUL FOR TODAY:

1.
2.
3.

TODAY"S PRIORITIES:

1.
2.
3.

THINGS I NEED TO DO FOR ME TODAY

1.
2.
3.

THINGS TO GET DONE:

Achieved? ✔

CLEAN:

PURCHASE:

DAILY HABITS I WANT
TO FORM:

Achieved? ✔

1.

2.

3.

4.

5.

3 PERSONAL WINS TODAY:

BRAIN DUMP & DAILY REFLECTION:

ABOUT THE AUTHOR

Tiana is CEO of **Rise N' Thrive**. Rise N' Thrive is a brand dedicated to helping people release self-doubt, build self-compassion, and embrace who they are so they can reach their full potential in life. She graduated from the University of North Texas with her Bachelors in Psychology and is an advocate for mental health awareness. She has spent her years working with youth organizations such as Girls Inc., YMCA, and Tarrant County Kids to promote mental health awareness and help teens learn to deal with the challenges and obstacles they may face in life in a healthy way.

Check out our Instagram **@riseandthrive_official** to get daily inspiration, self-care tips and tricks, and motivation.

Also check out our daily planner ***Calming the Chaos*** available on Amazon!